I0494564

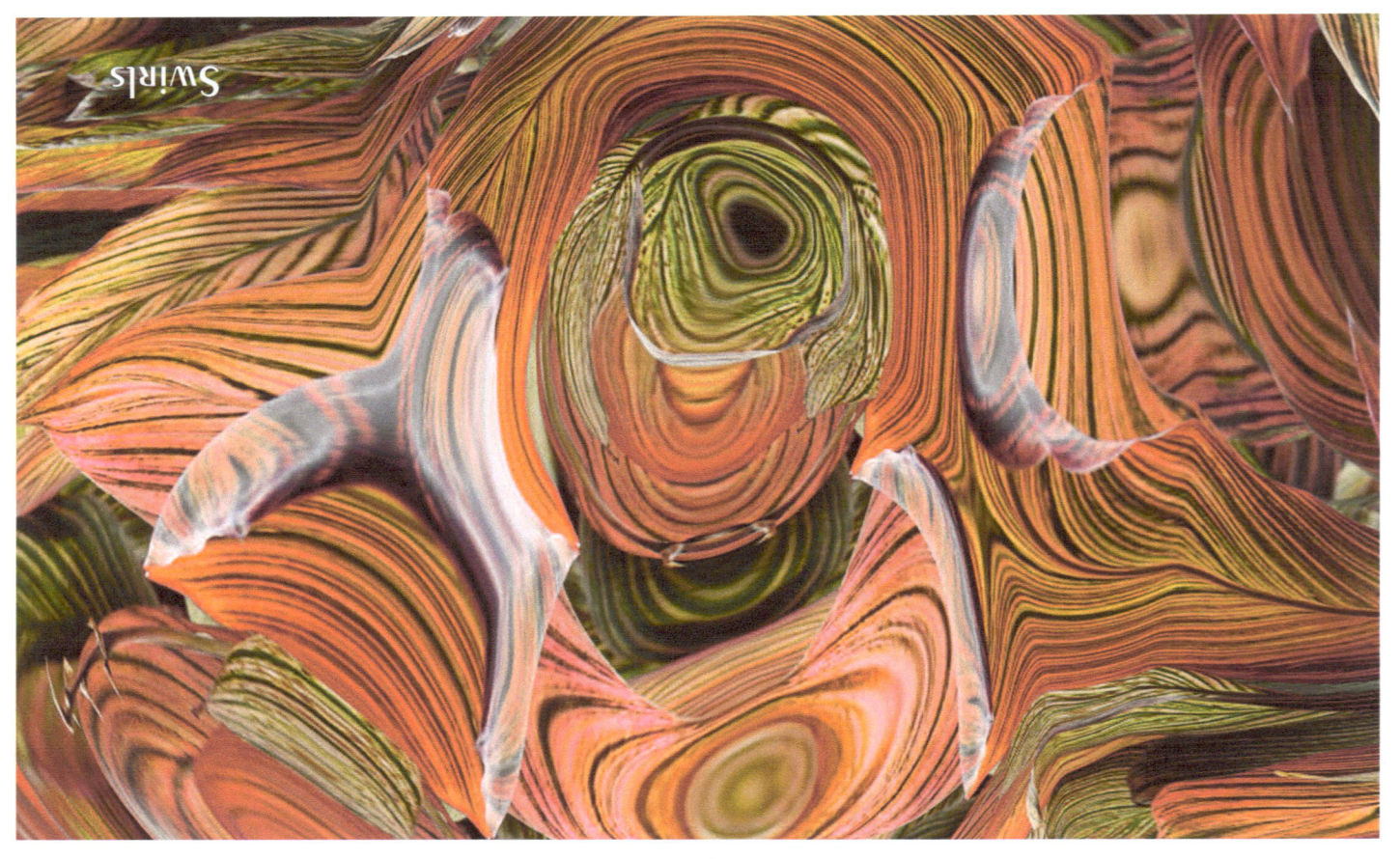

Swirls

Creative Art

Creative Art

Klaus D. Emrich

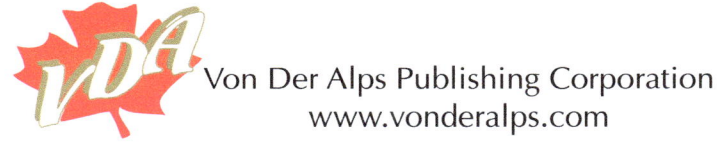
Von Der Alps Publishing Corporation
www.vonderalps.com

Creative Art

by Klaus D. Emrich

.

Copyright and Intellectual/Creative Property of the author/photographer/artist, Klaus D. Emrich
starting with © 2014 and beyond.

First original published in April 2014 by
Von Der Alps Publishing Corporation
CANADA

www.vonderalps.com

All rights reserved

This publication is the original Literary Work, Creative ART and Photography
of author/artist/photographer Klaus D. Emrich,
protected under the Canadian and International Copyright Agreements.
It cannot be reproduced, recorded or transmitted by any means, without permission from the author.

Canadian Cataloguing in Publication Data

ISBN 978-0-9782302-9-6

Printed in USA

Creative Art

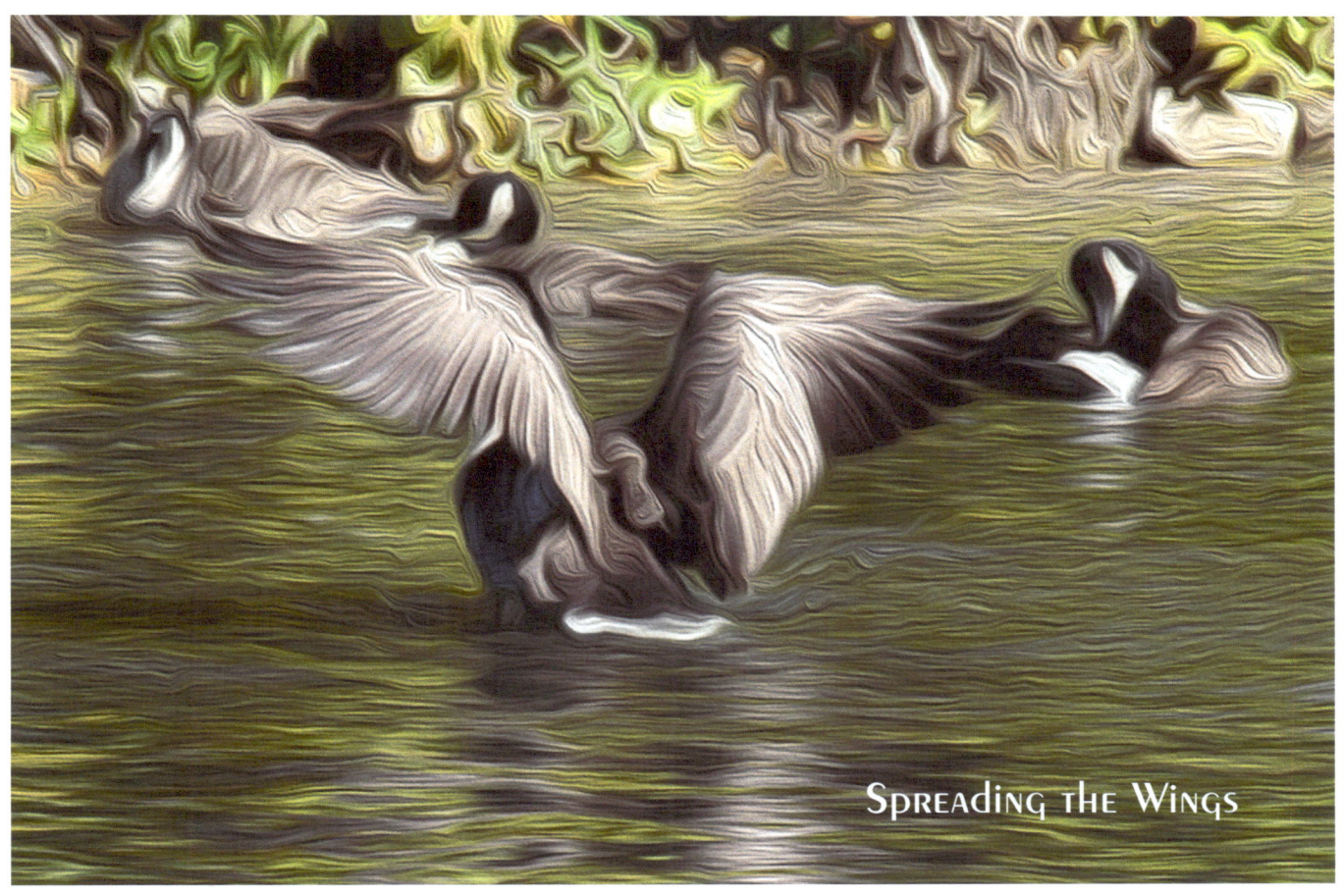

Spreading the Wings

Creative Art

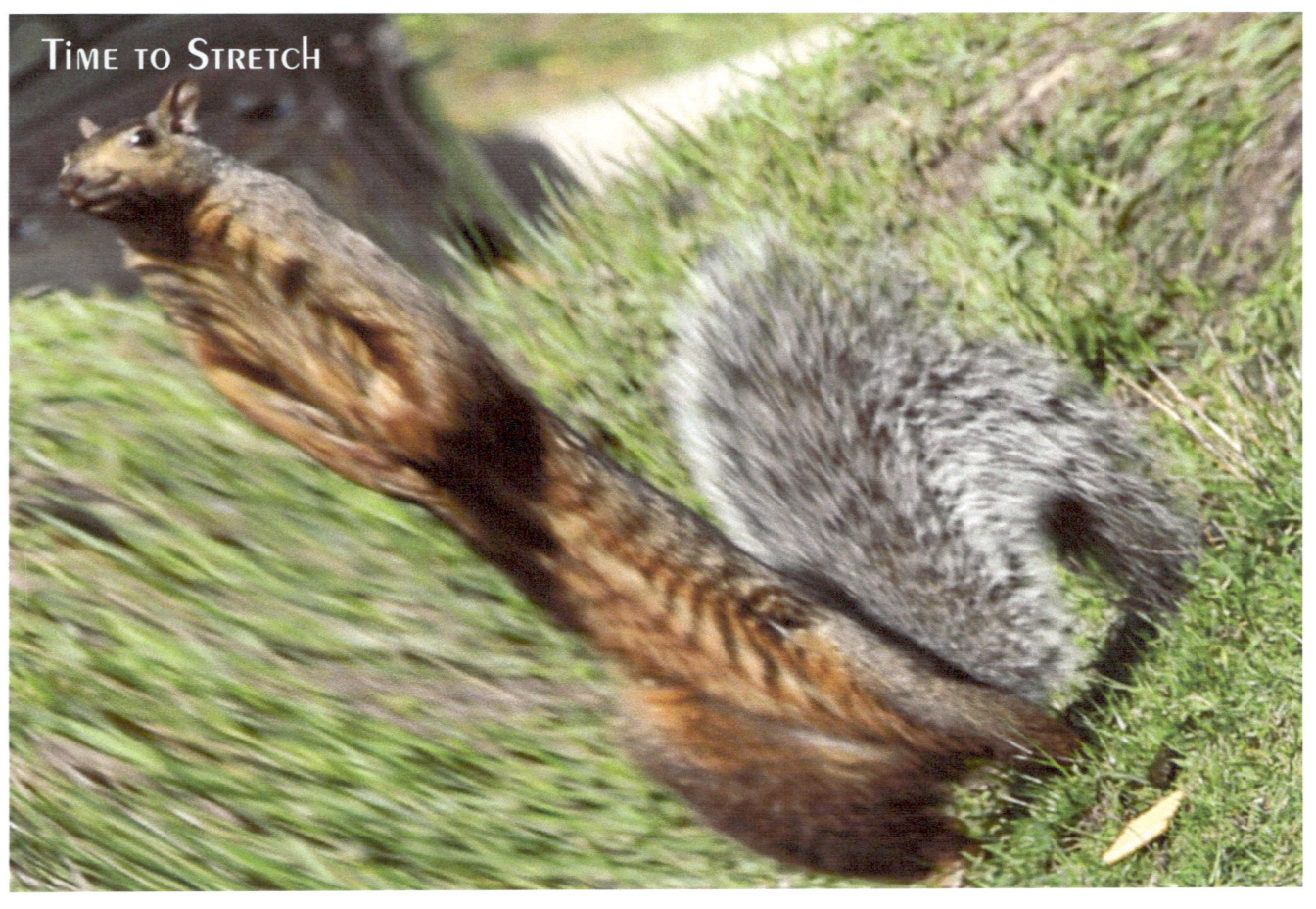

TIME TO STRETCH

Creative Art

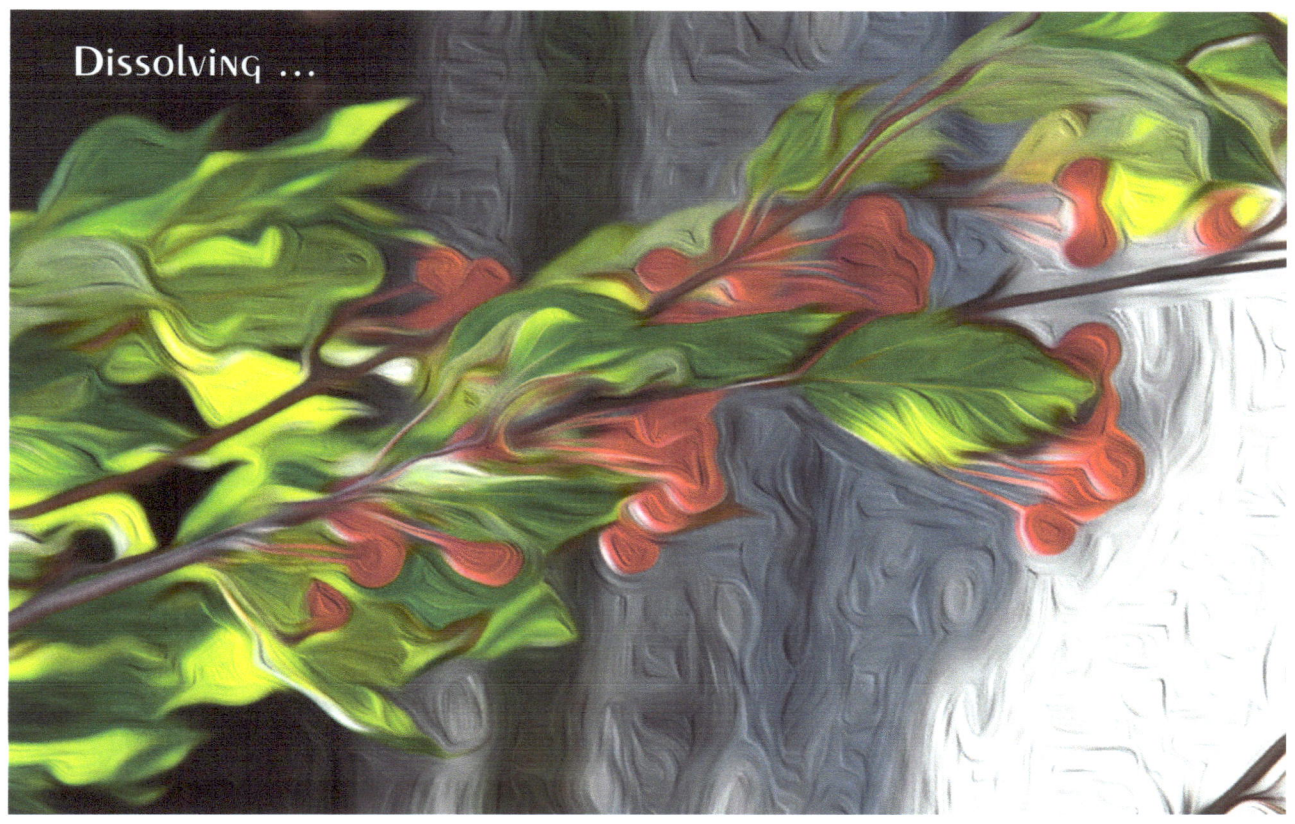

Dissolving …

Creative Art

A Place to Relax

Creative Art

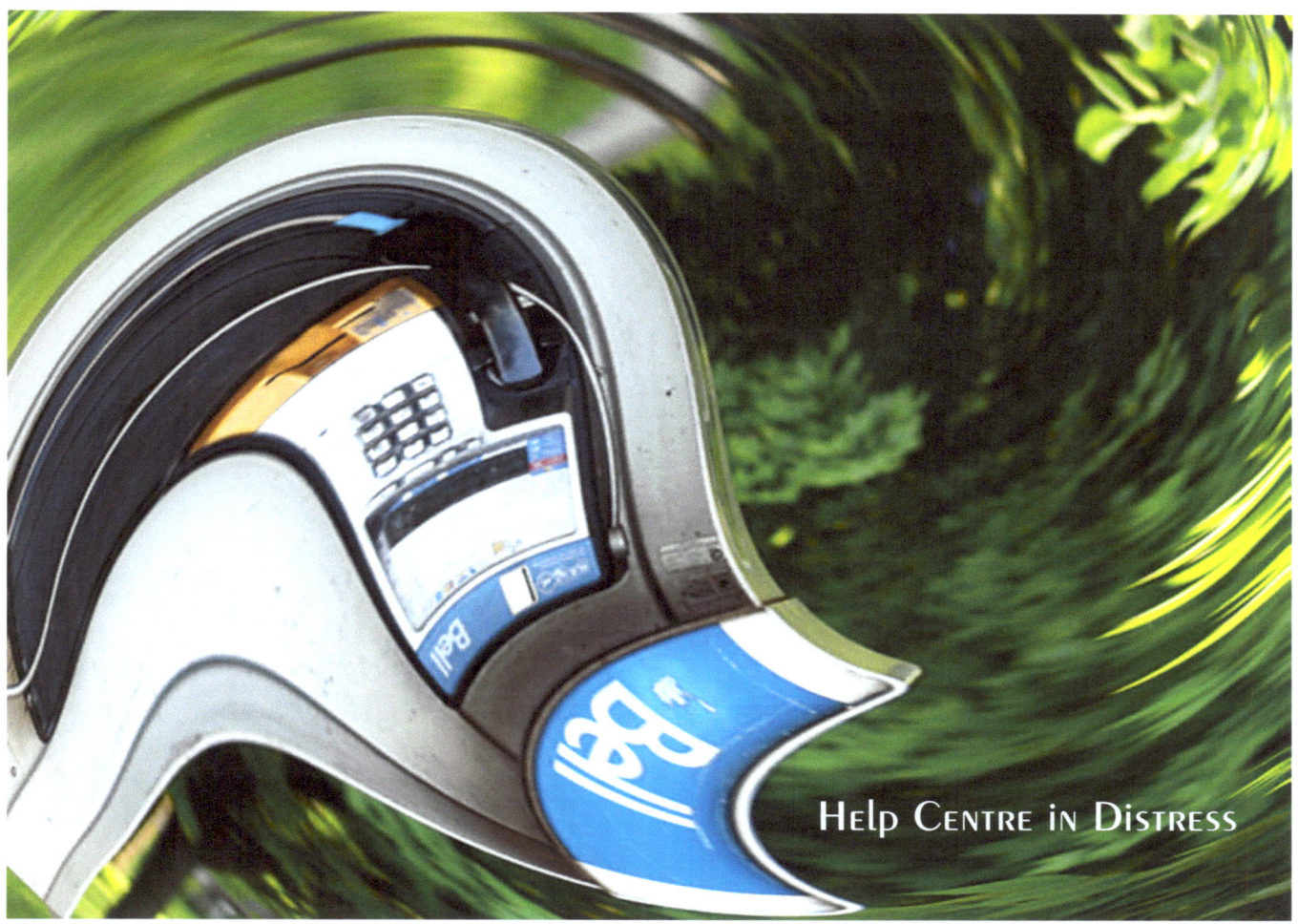

Help Centre in Distress

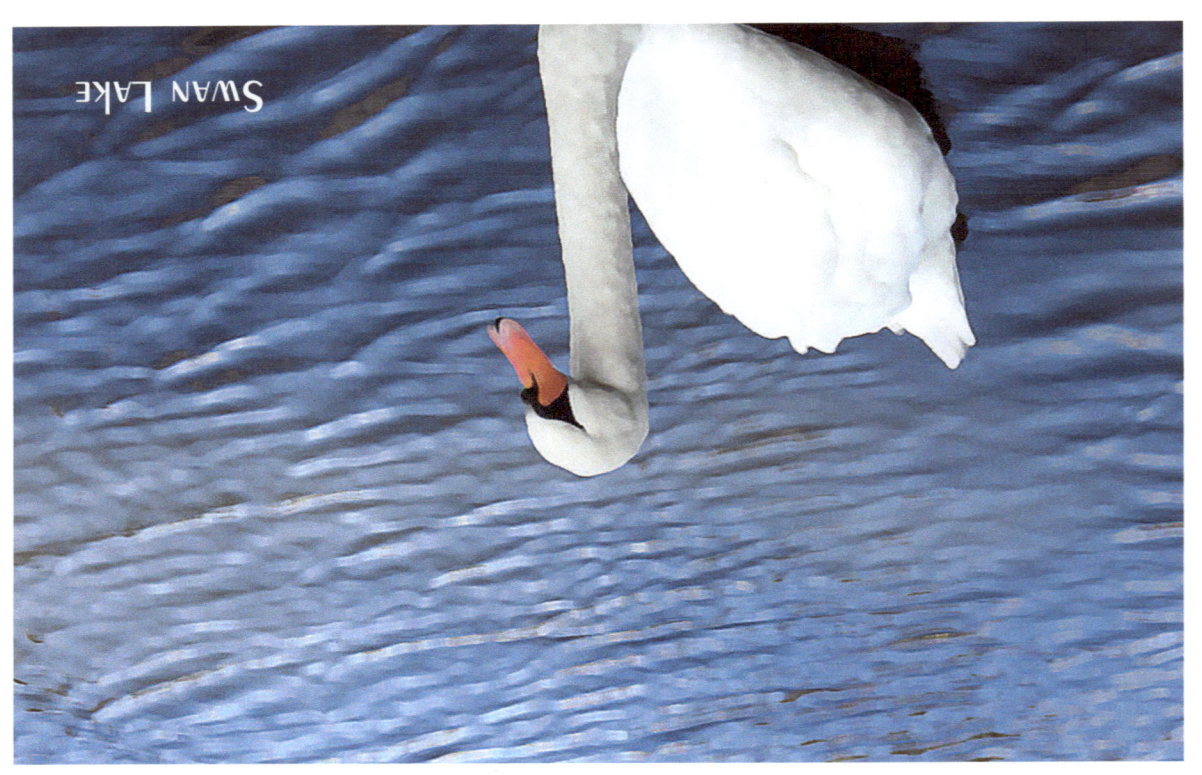

Swan Lake

Creative Art

Creative Art

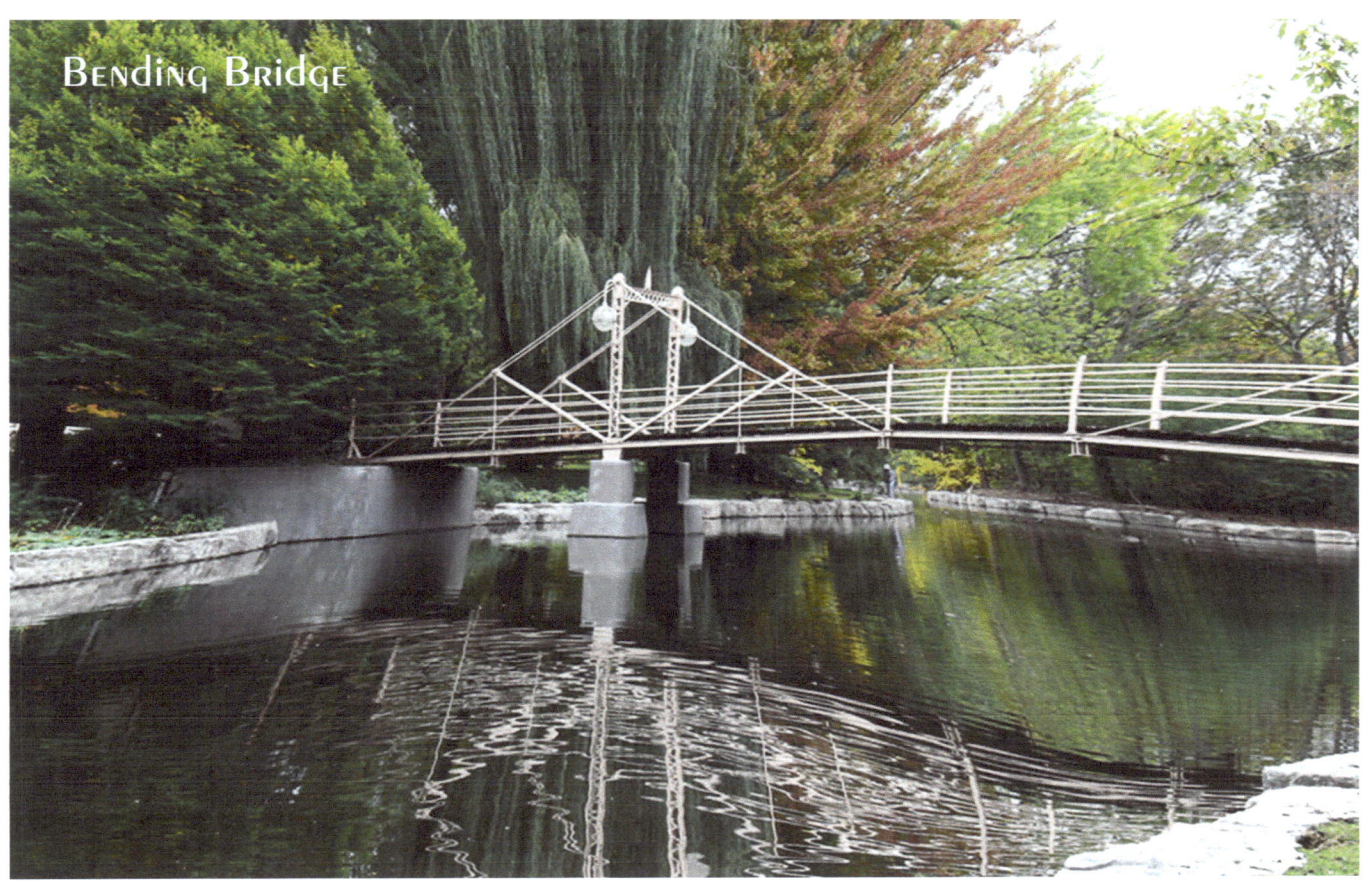

Bending Bridge

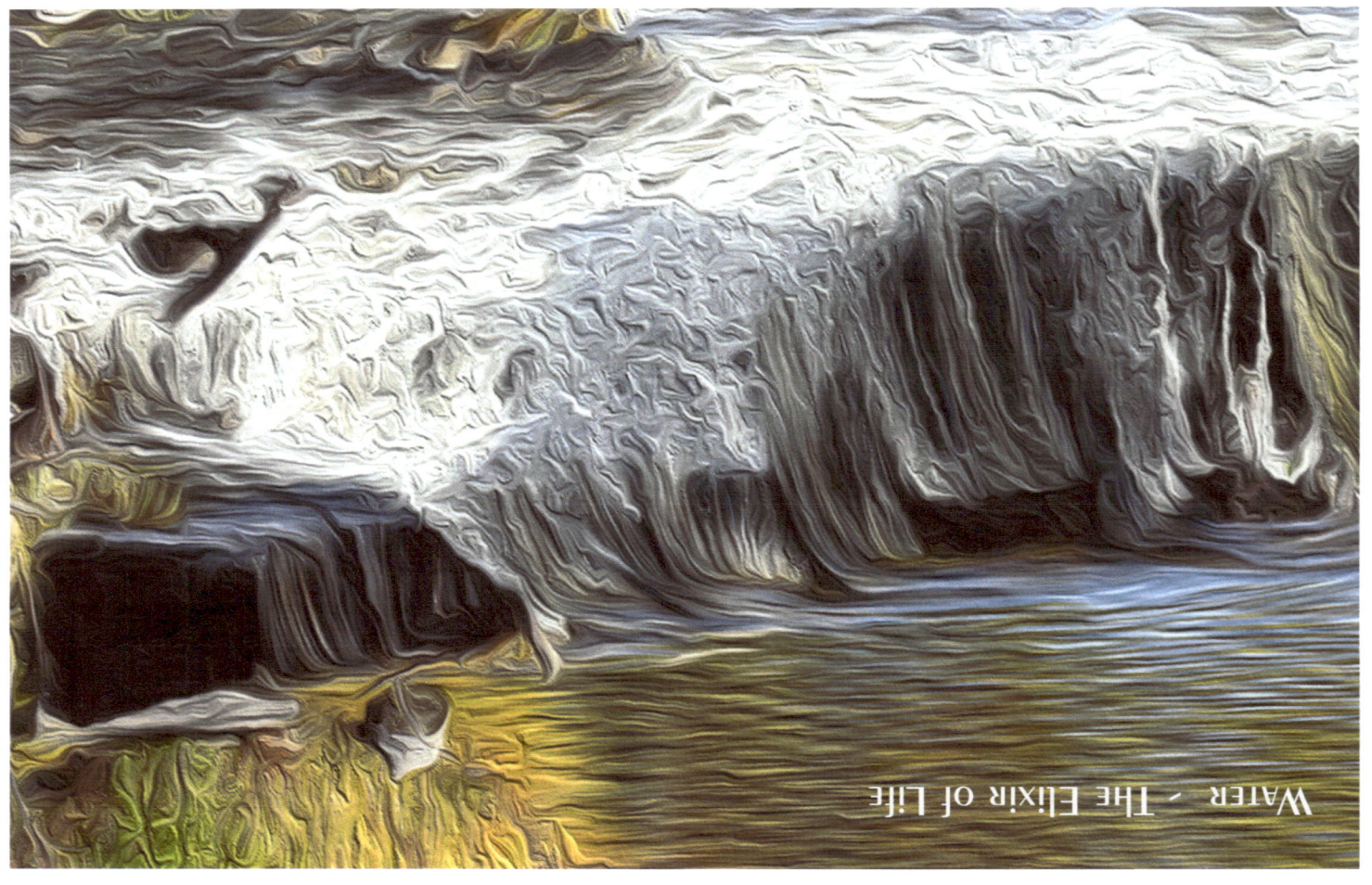

Water – The Elixir of Life

Creative Art

Creative Art

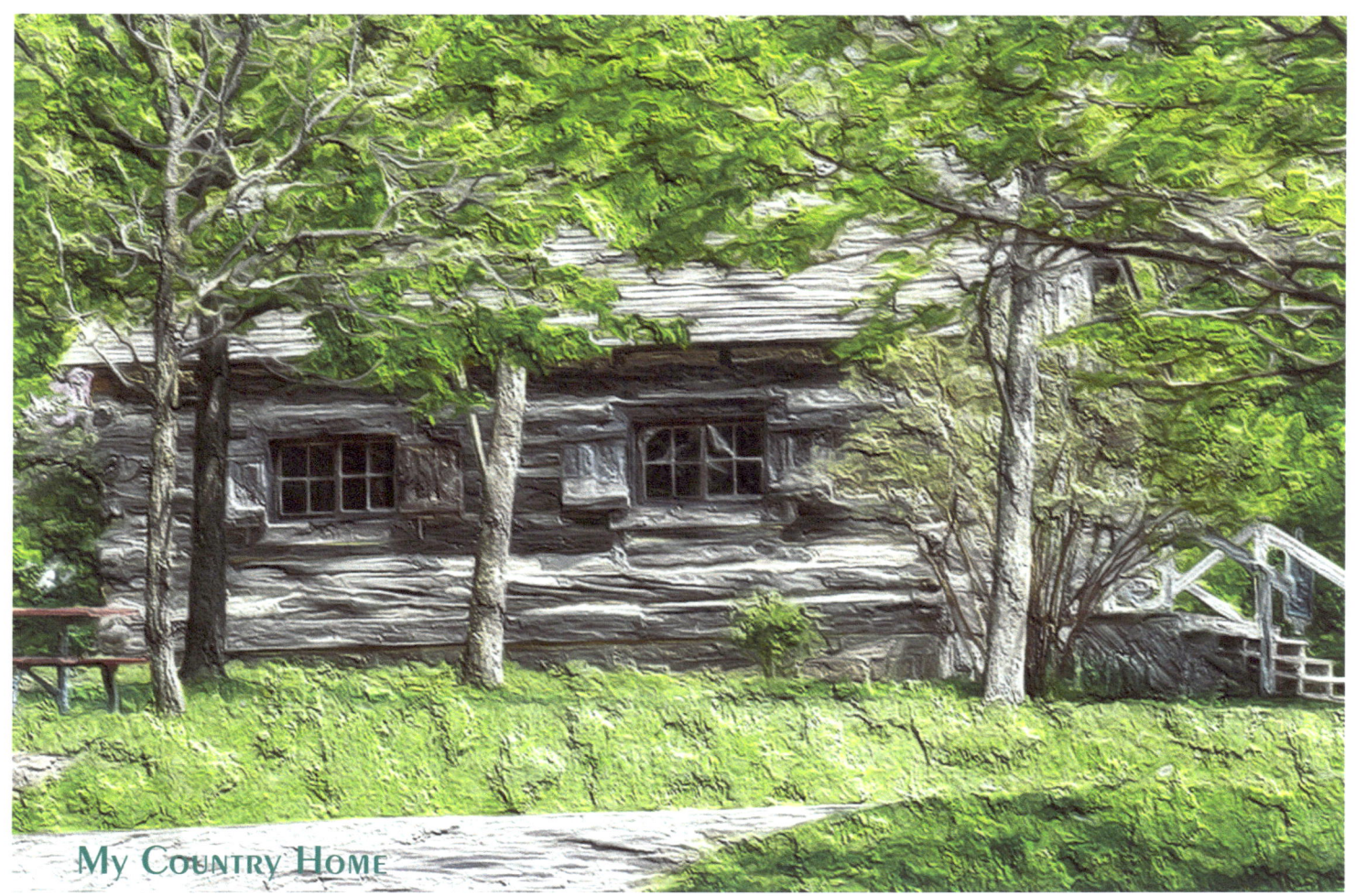

My Country Home

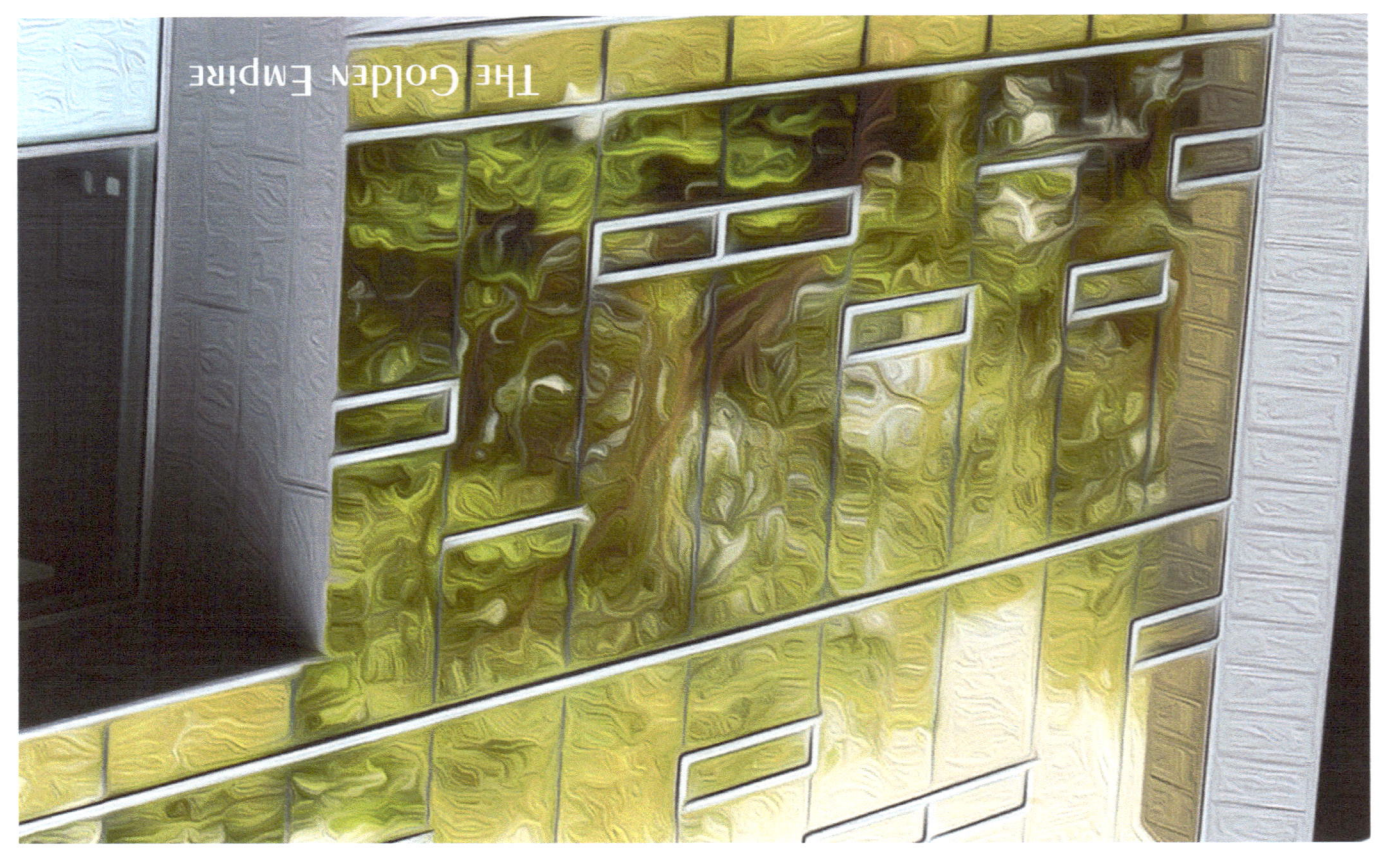

The Golden Empire

Creative Art

Creative Art

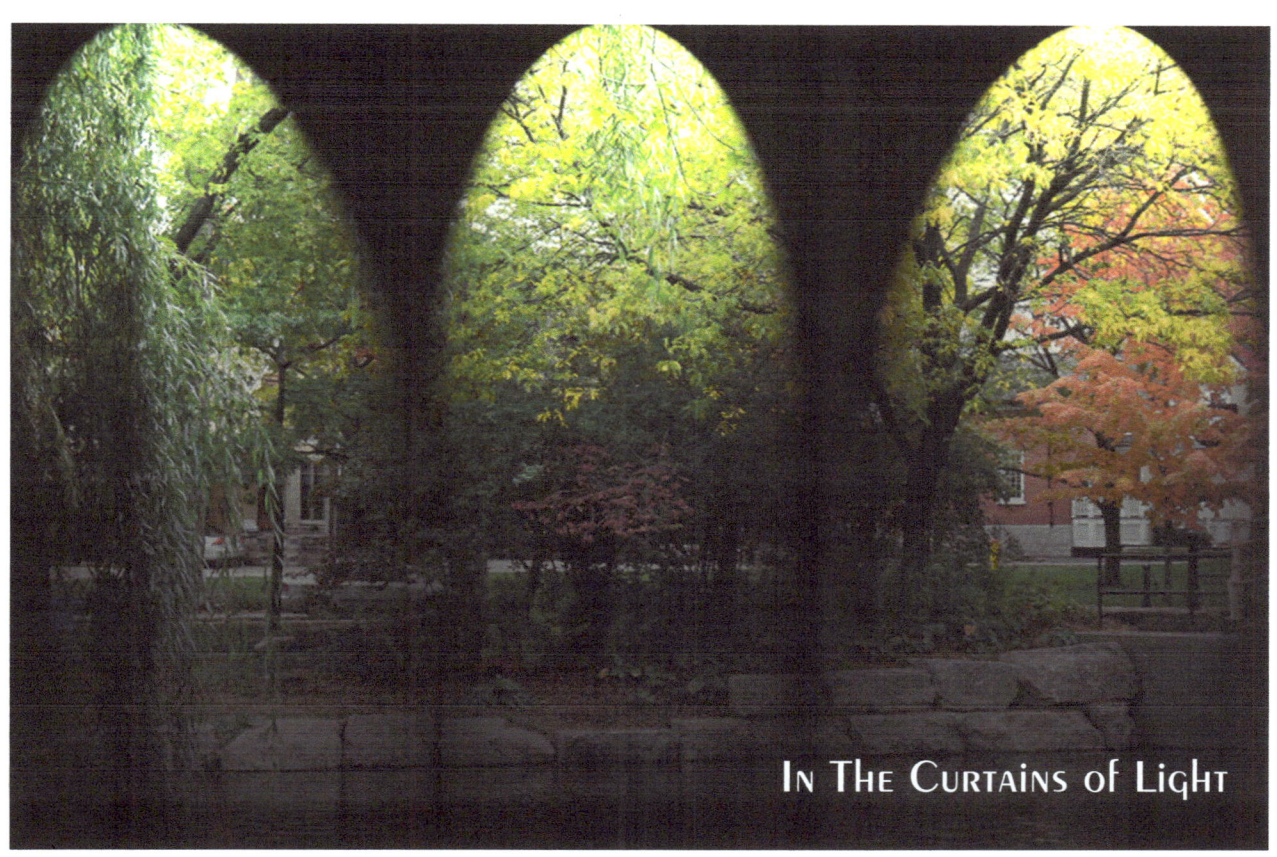

In The Curtains of Light

Creative Art

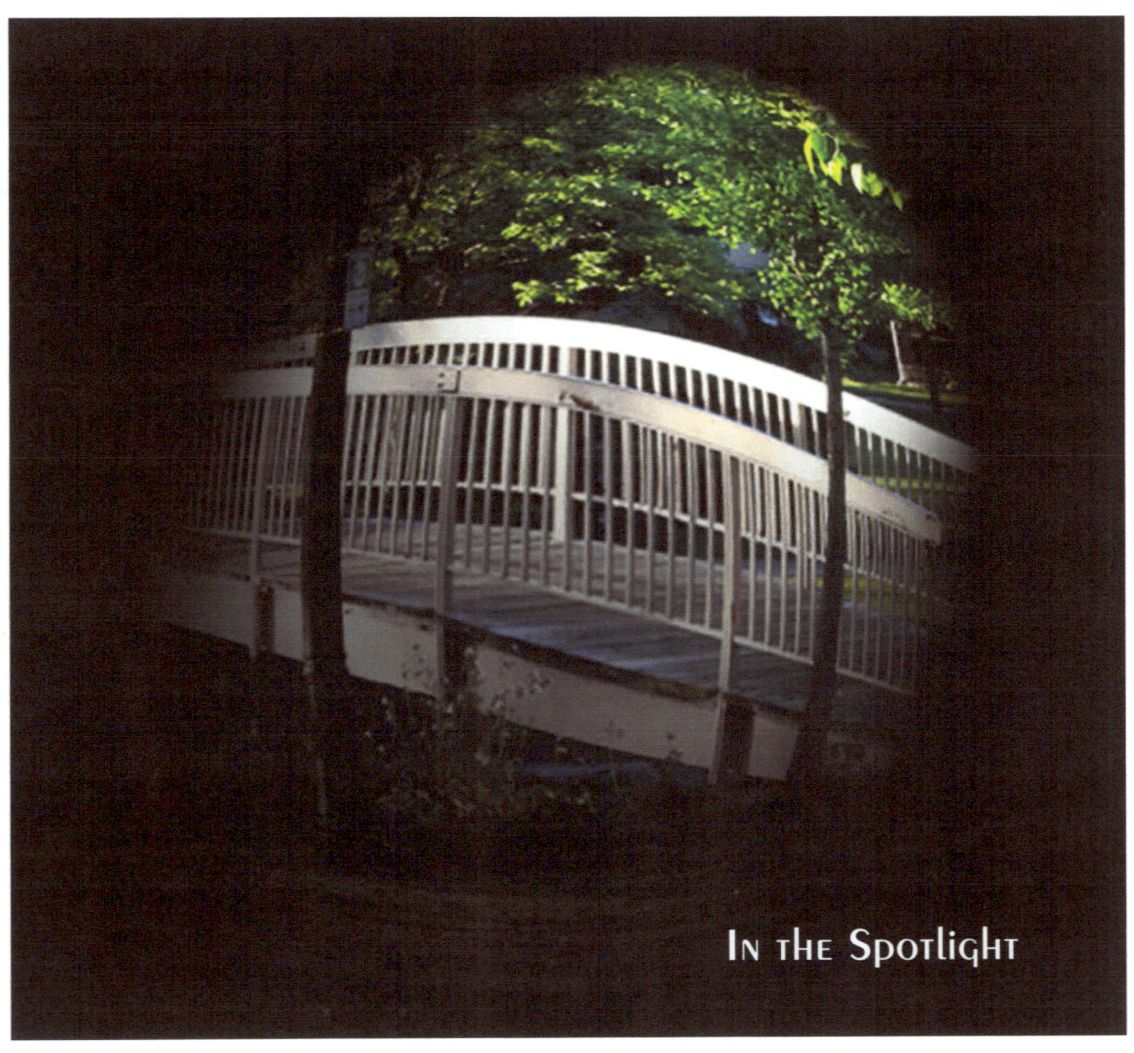

In the Spotlight

Creative Art

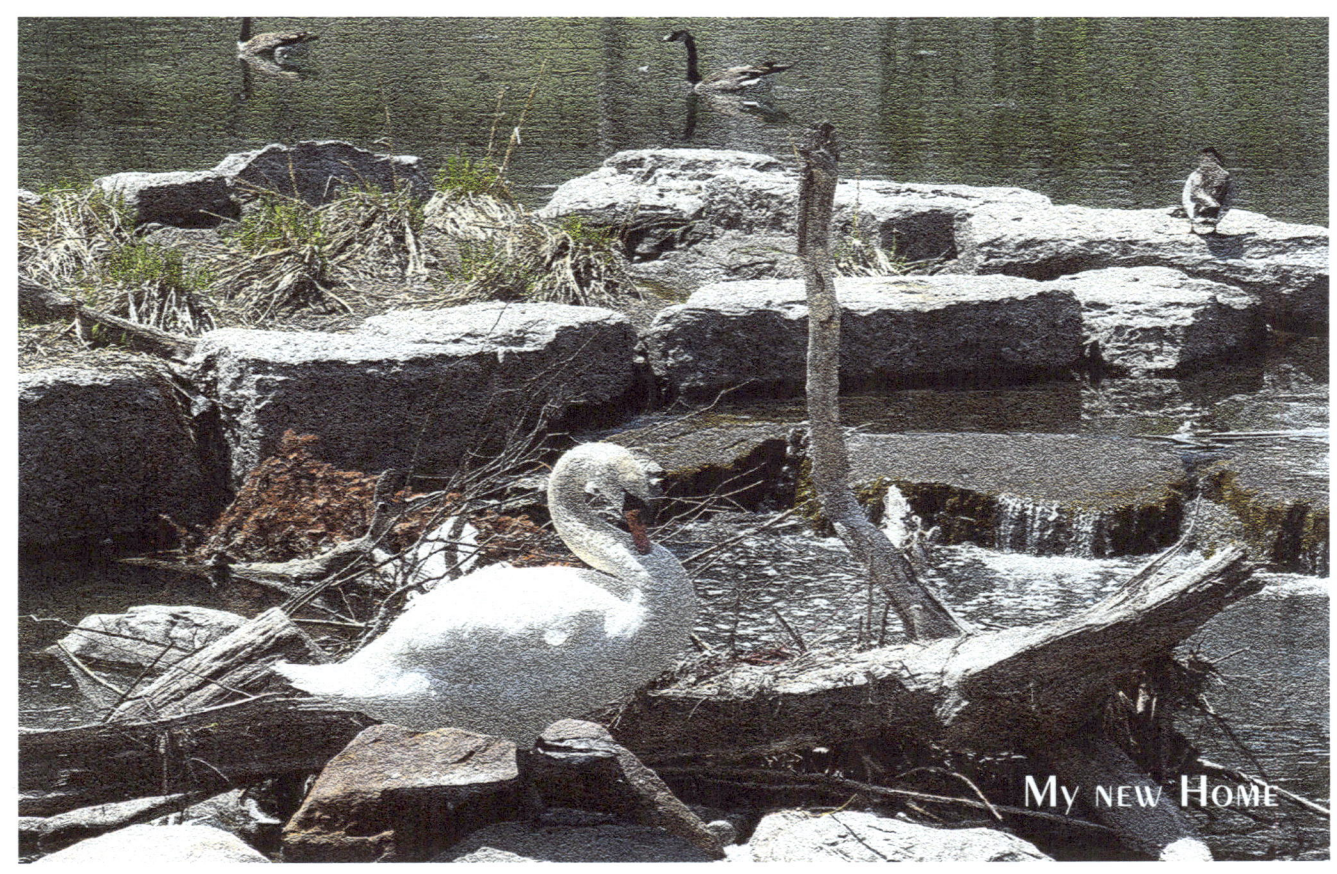

My new Home

Creative Art

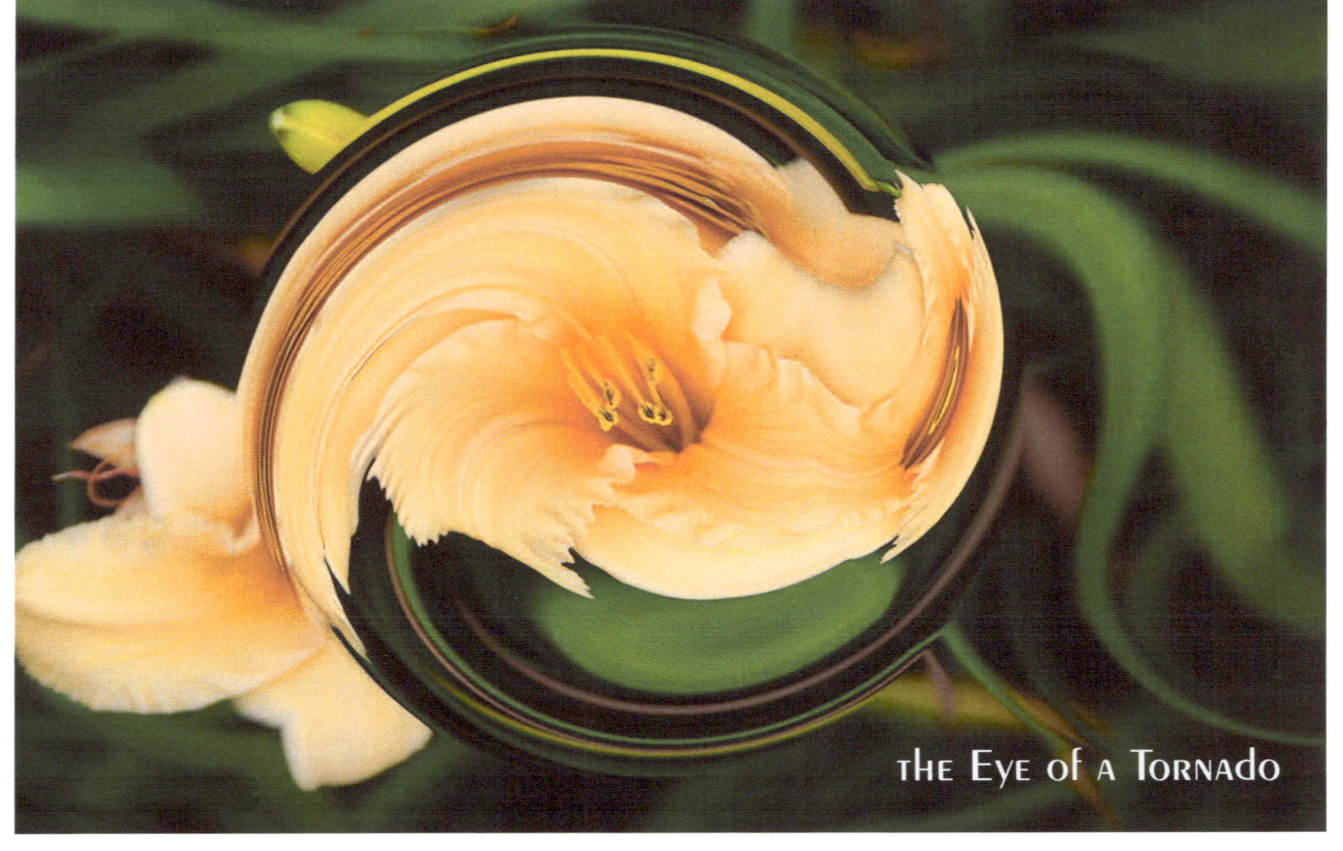

THE Eye of a Tornado

Creative Art

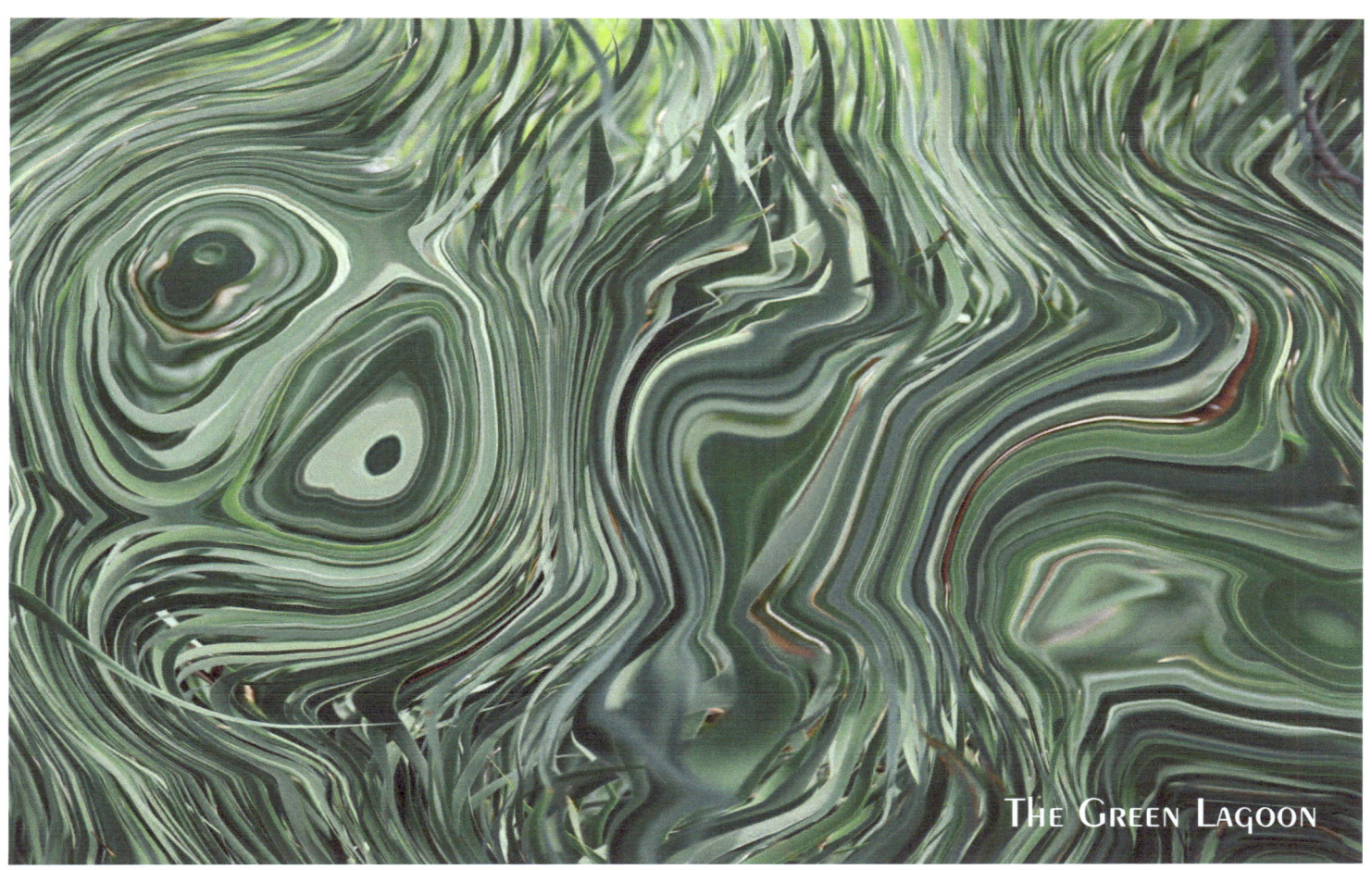

THE GREEN LAGOON

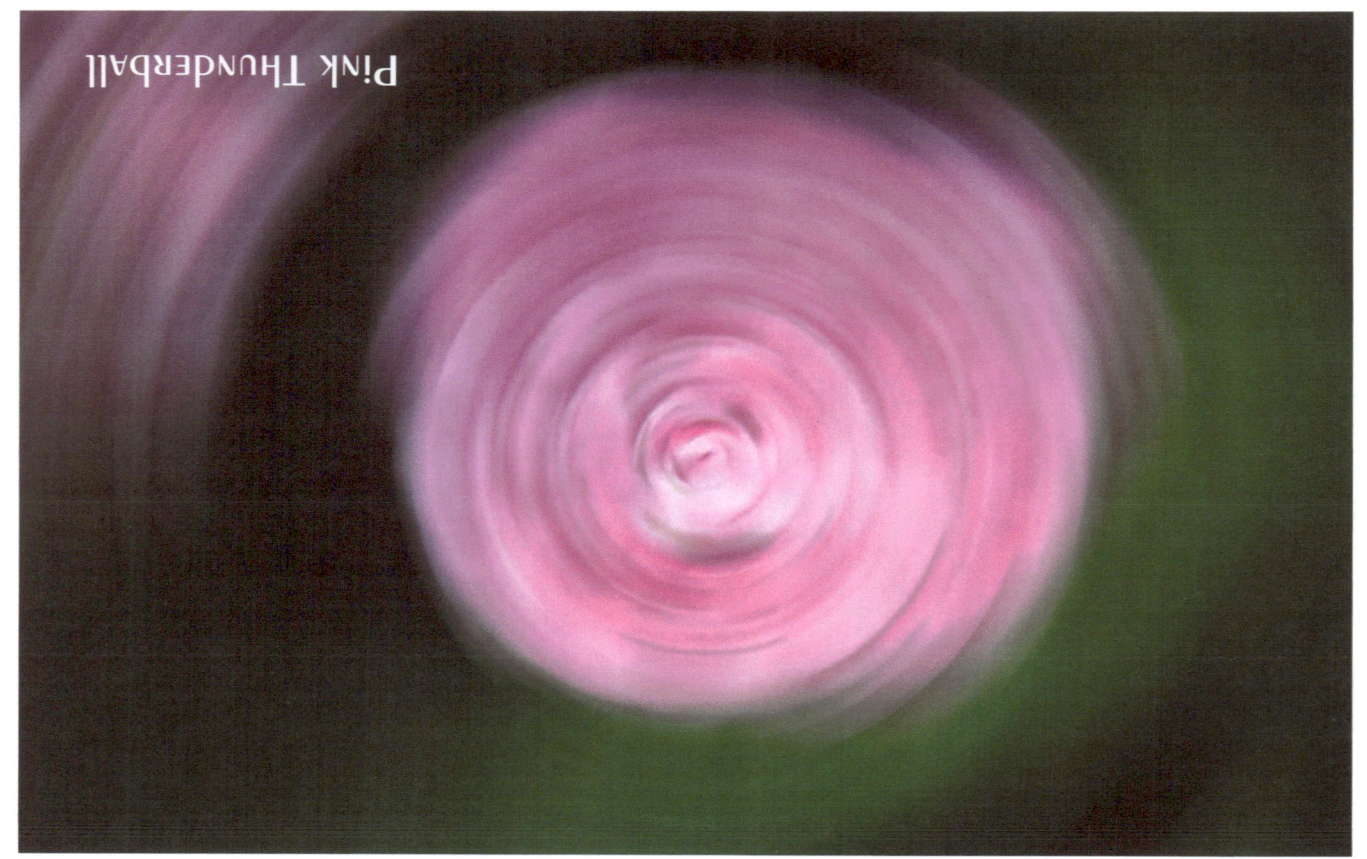

Pink Thunderball

Creative Art

Creative Art

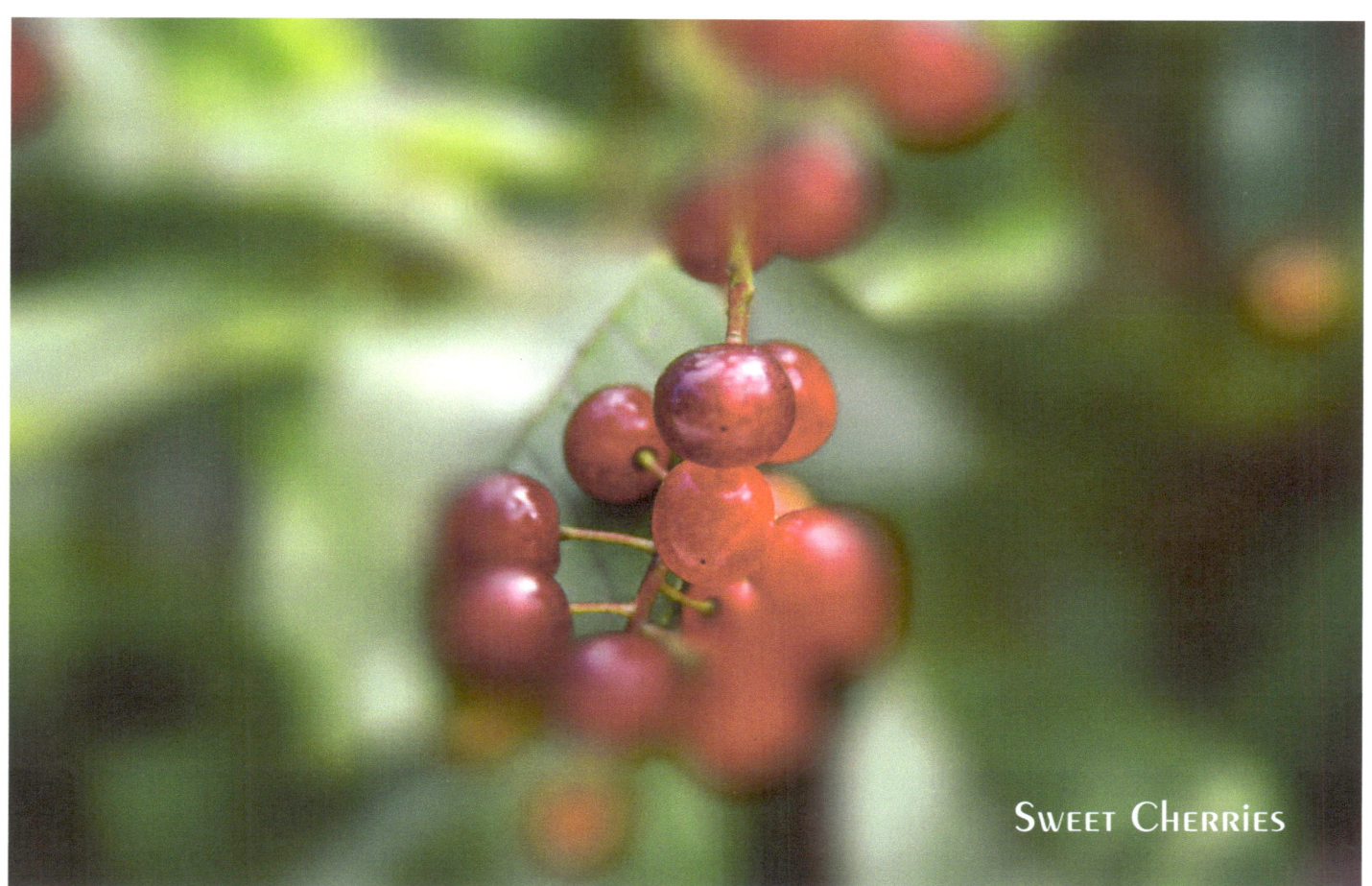

SWEET CHERRIES

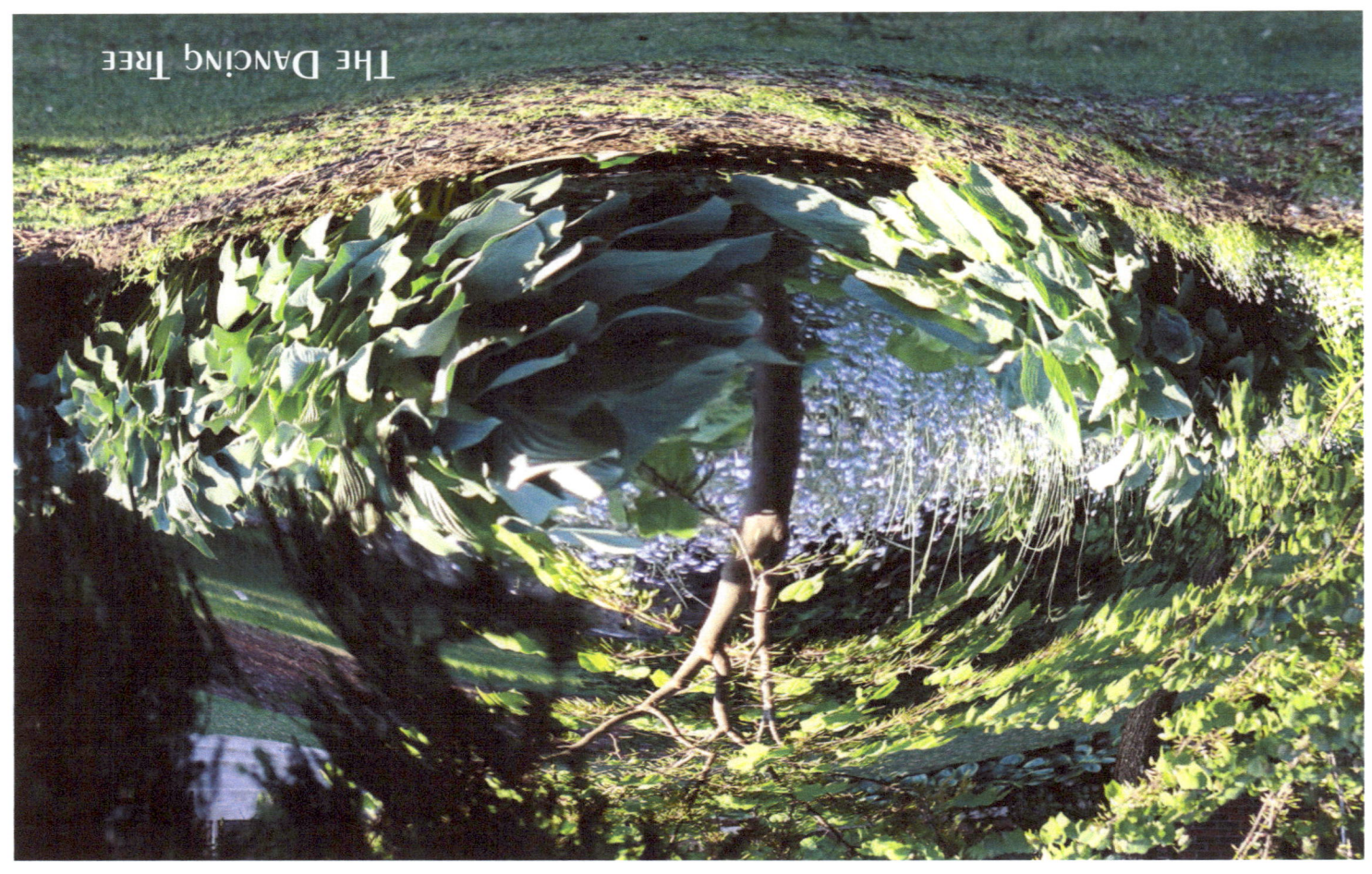

The Dancing Tree

Creative Art

Creative Art

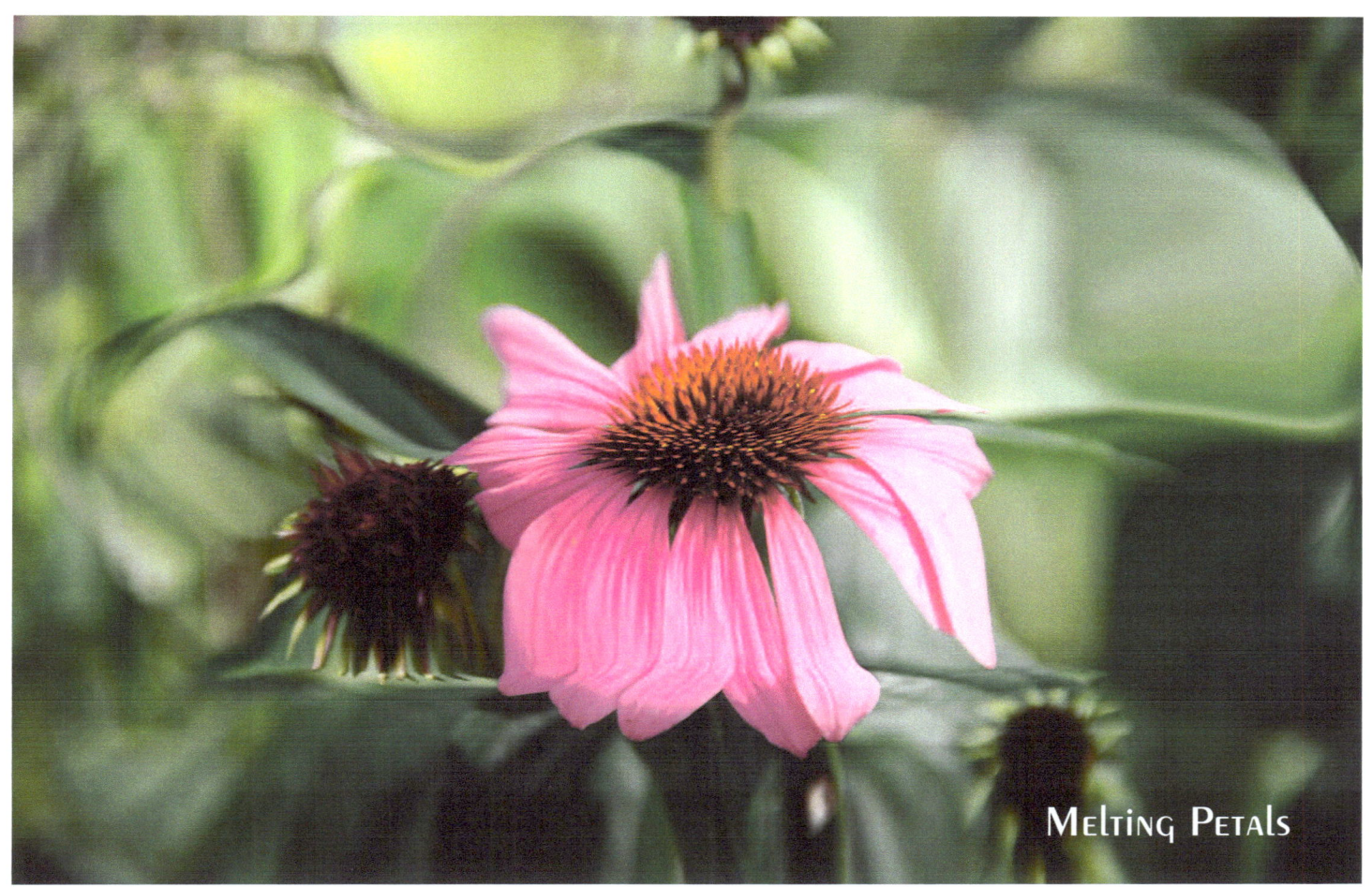

Melting Petals

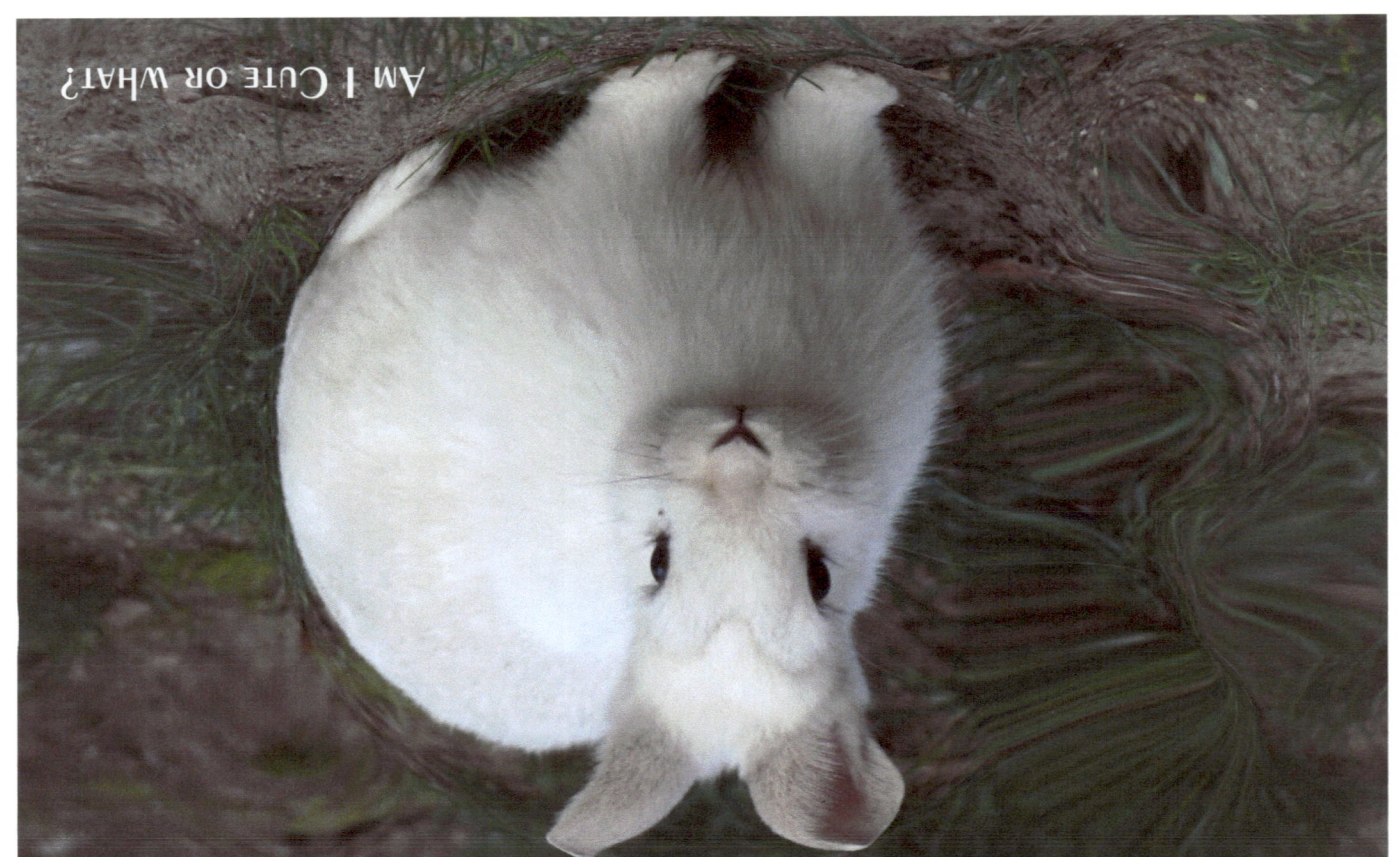

Am I Cute or What?

Creative Art

Creative Art

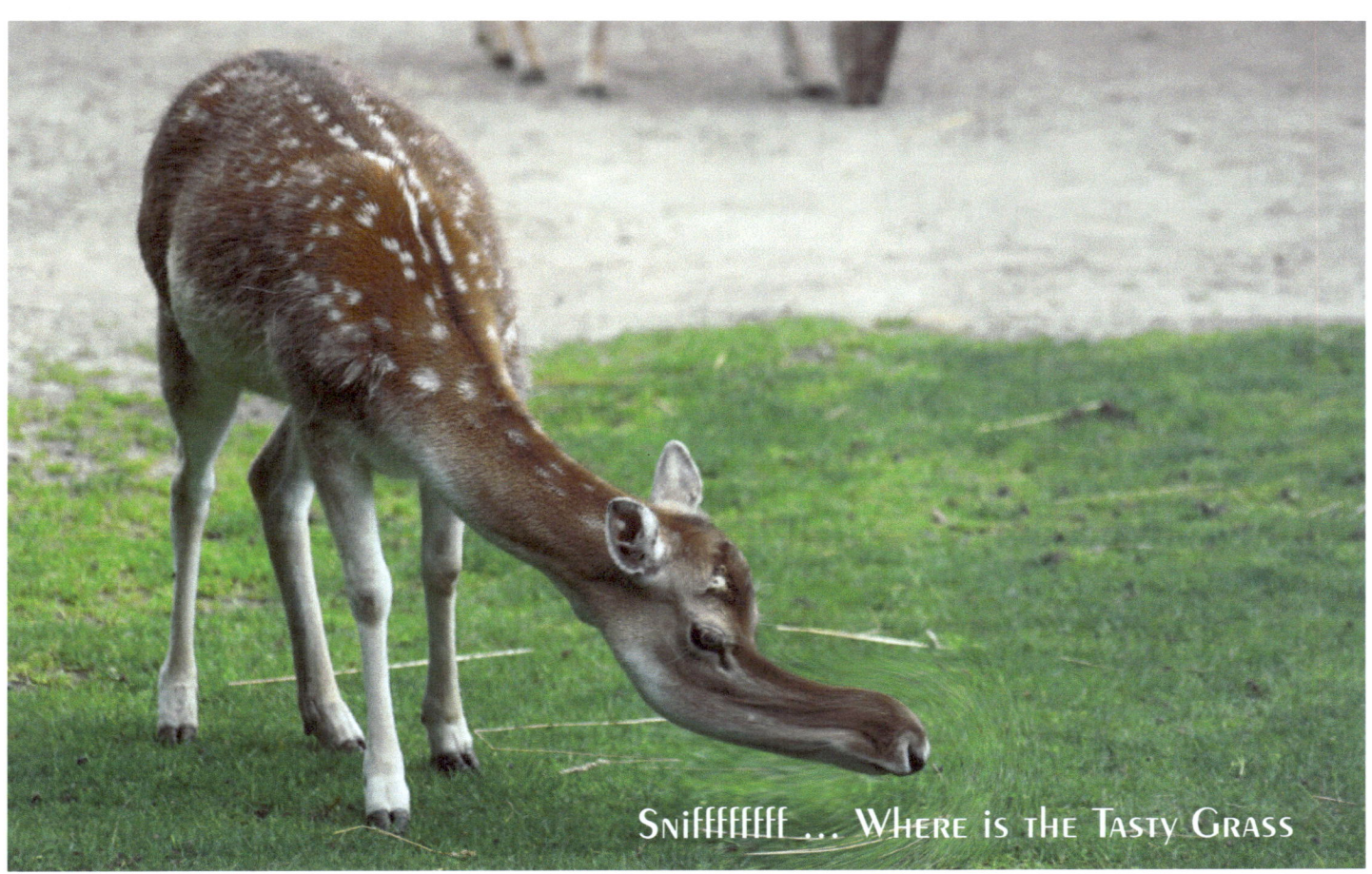

Snifffffffff ... Where is the Tasty Grass

Creative Art

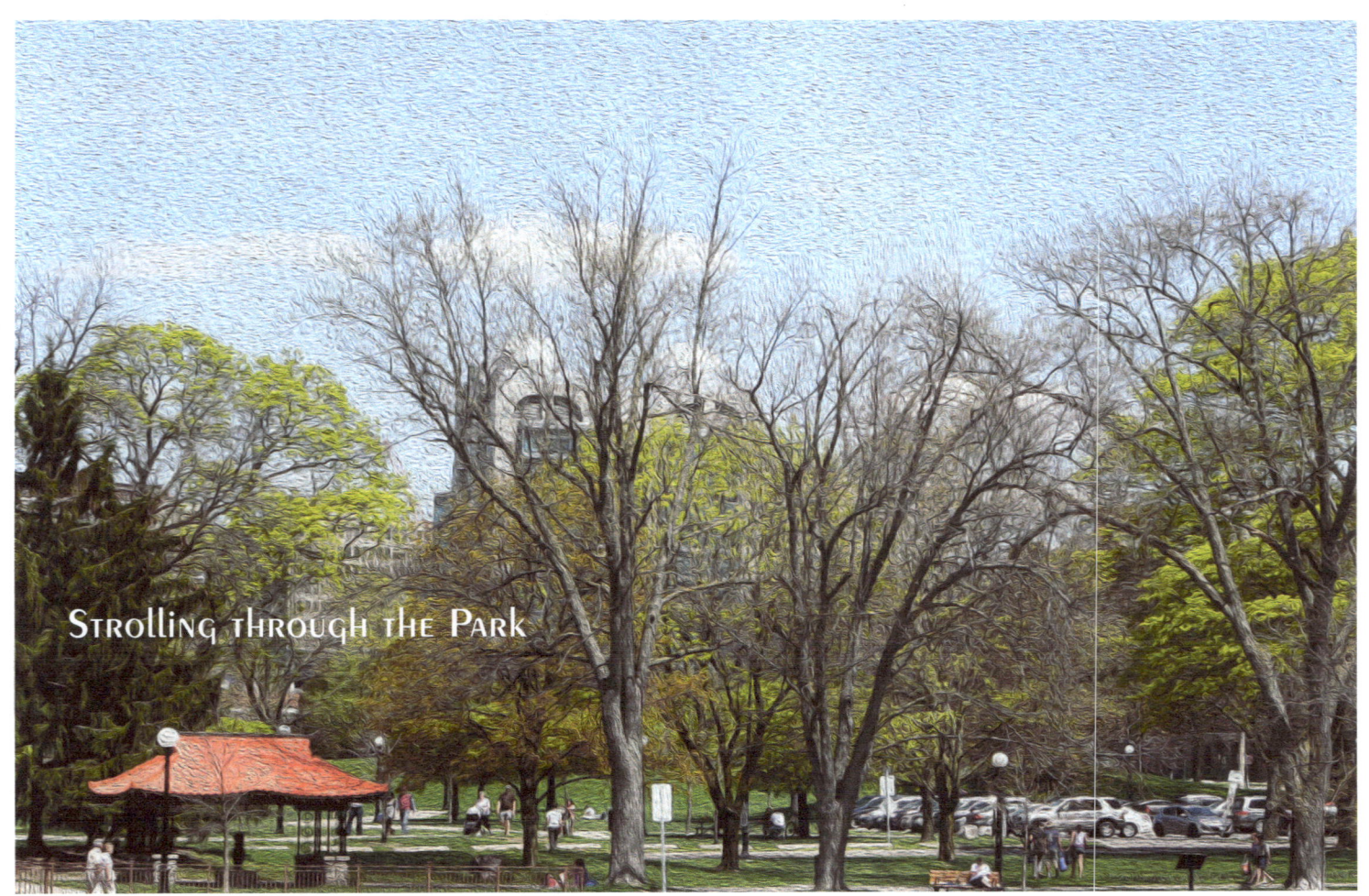

Strolling through the Park

Creative Art

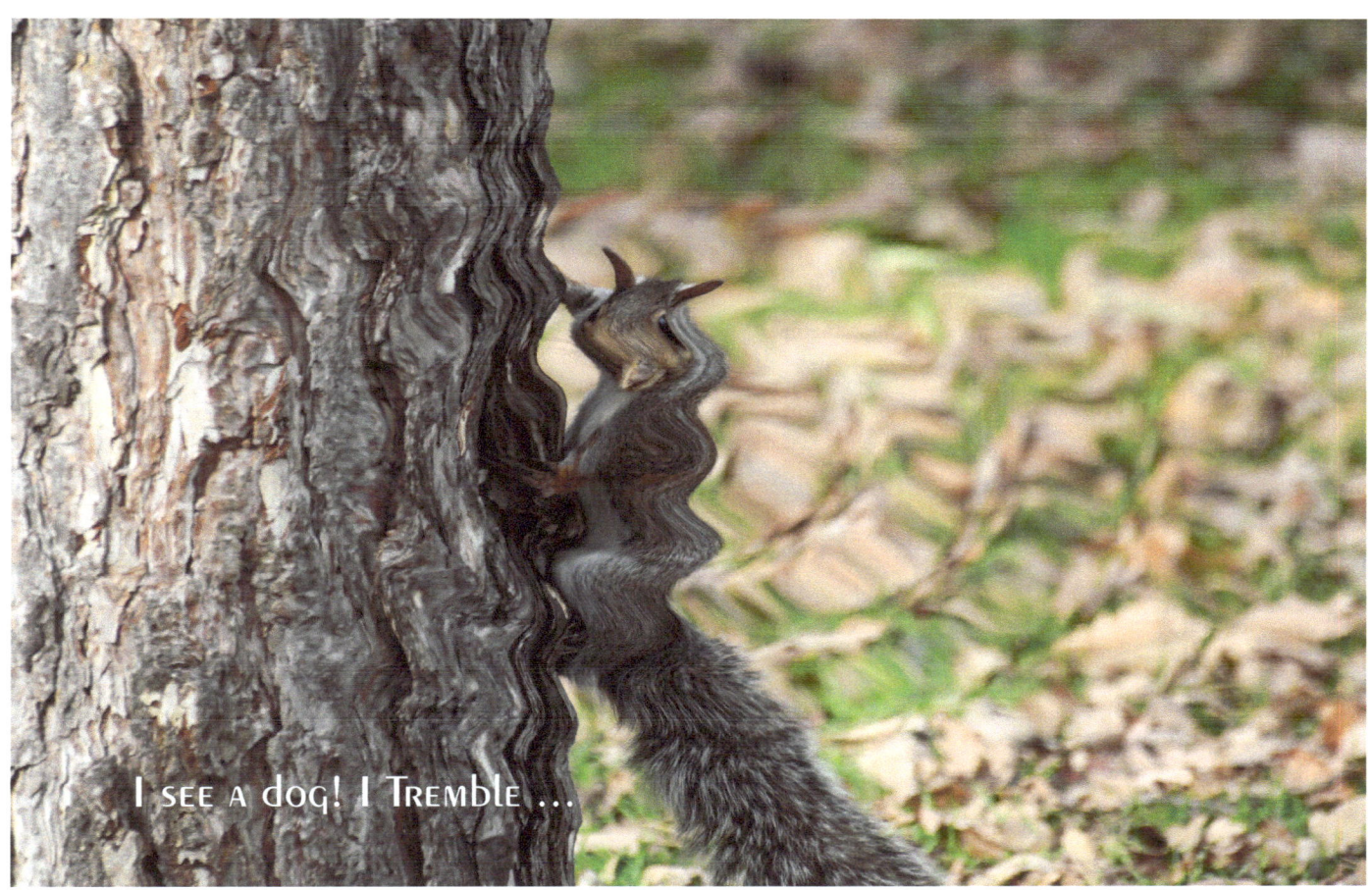

I see a dog! I Tremble ...

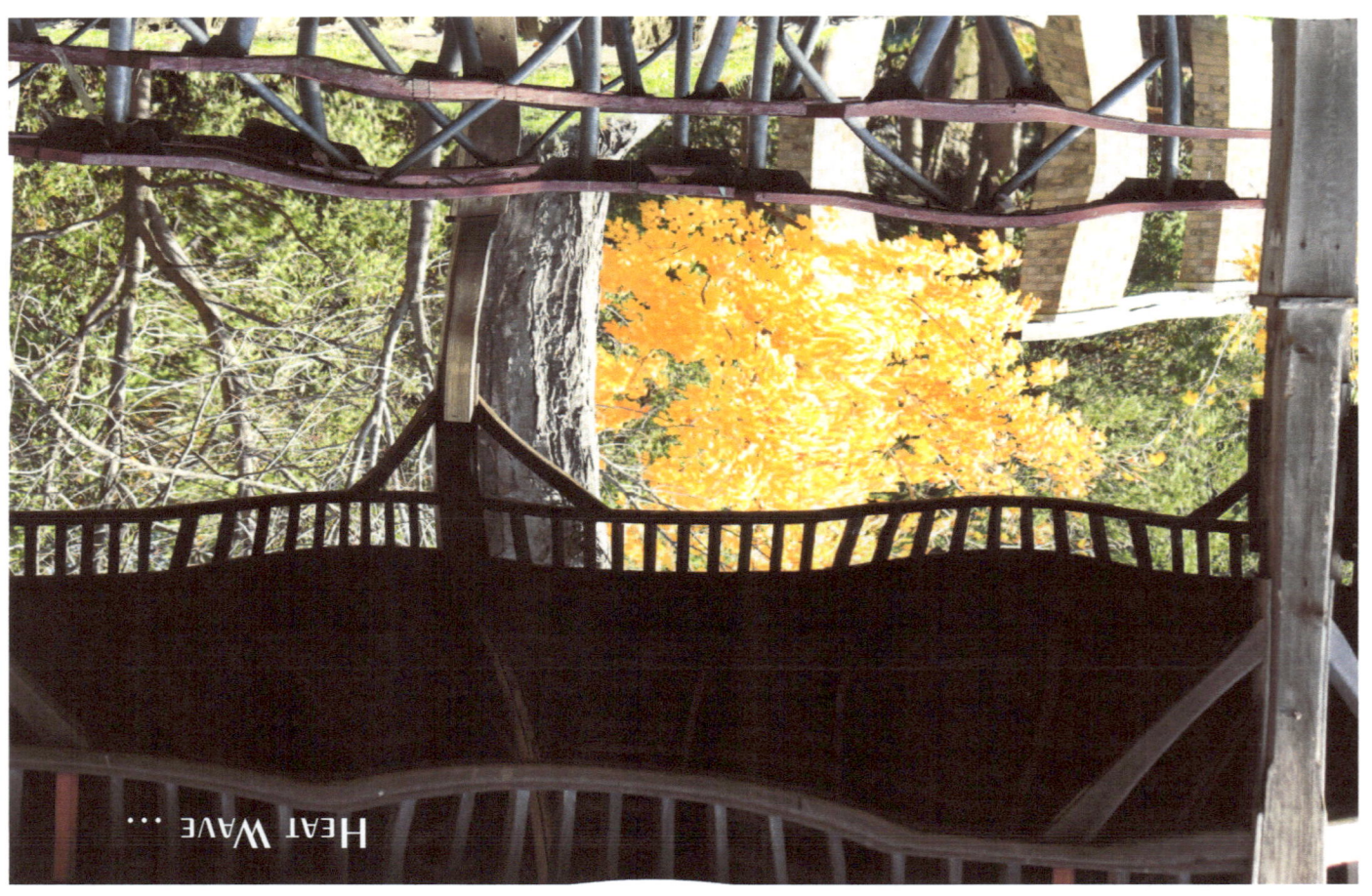

Heat Wave ...

Creative Art

Creative Art

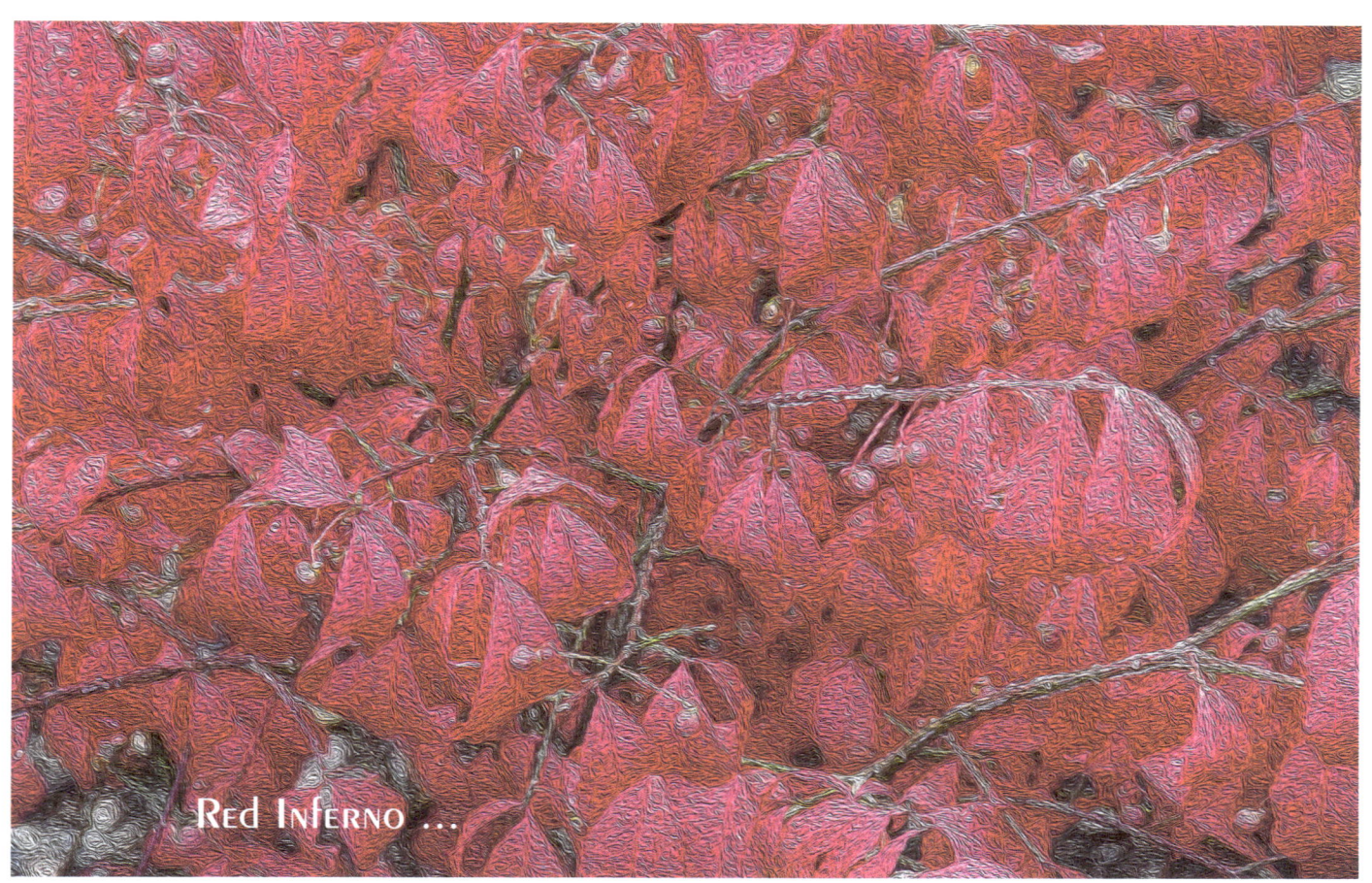

Red Inferno ...

Bibliography—Klaus D. Emrich

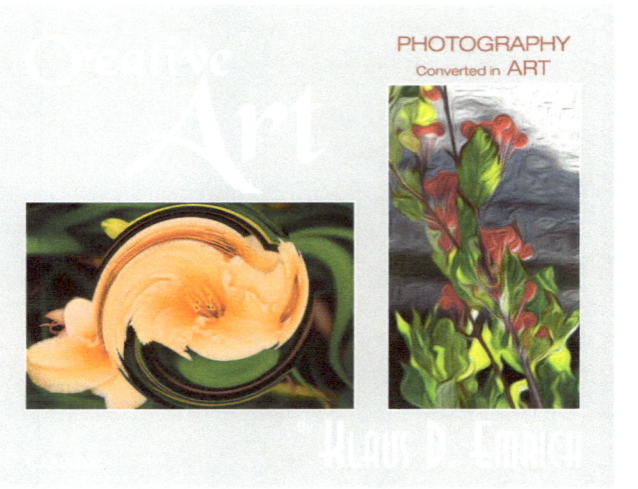

Books also available in German Language.

Creative Art
Artistic view via photography.

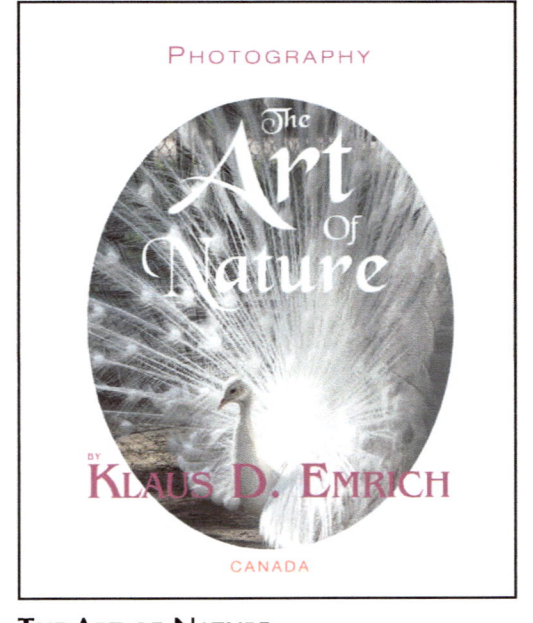

The Art of Nature
Photography - Canadian nature

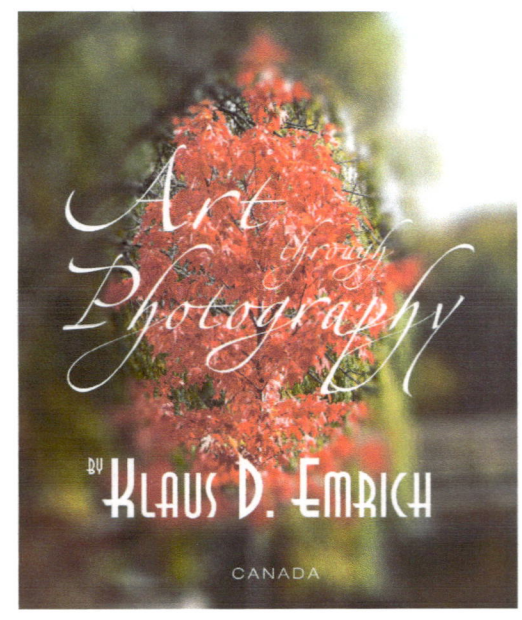

Art through Photography
Photography converted into art.

The squirrels and I
Photographed story.

About the Artist

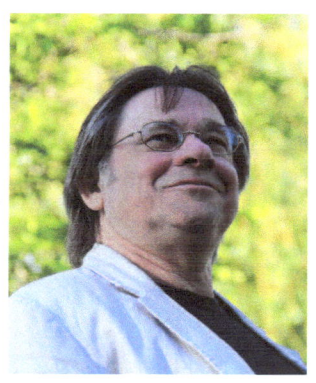

Klaus D. Emrich loved art since he was a small child growing up near Frankfurt am Main, Germany. Often, he would go out in nature's fields to sketch or paint. Extremely attracted to the multitude of beauty all around, in recent years Klaus started using his artistic talent via modern options.

Creating beauty was always his greatest dream. "Creative Art," published in 2014 by Von Der Alps Publishing Corporation, is Klaus' second book (with many more to come).

Klaus D. Emrich and his wife Mary Emrich, (Award Winning author/poet/photographer of multiple books on Amazon, under the pseudonym Elysse Poetis) reside in the famous Region of Waterloo, Ontario - a wonderful North American continental place named "The Quantum Valley of CANADA."

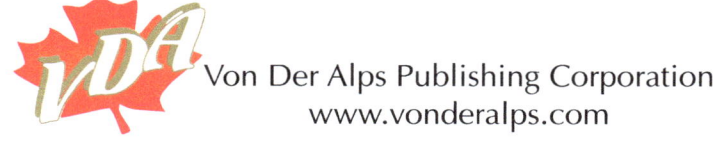
Von Der Alps Publishing Corporation
www.vonderalps.com

www.ingramcontent.com/pod-product-compliance
Lightning Source LLC
Chambersburg PA
CBHW050416180526
45159CB00005B/2293